#1 COMMENTS

CHAMPION:

He/She provides the resources and the climate for problem solving.

TEAM FORMATION:

Consider all affected activities

    Sub Suppliers of components
    Raw Material Sources

    Purchased services sources

    Customer

    Machine Builder

    Gage and/or test equipment supplier

    Inside/Outside experts

    Packaging Engineers

    Others

The magnitude of the problem may dictate the depth of the brainstorming phase.

Obtain the "Buy-in" of each participating activity.

GOALS – Define the 8D team goals in writing as an initial team activity. Obtain group consensus.

RULES – Clearly define the team rules.

    #1 – NO CRITICISM – Everyone's opinion is important

    #2 – EVERYONE CONTRIBUTES – it is ok to "pass," but each team member must participate.

#2   EXAMPLE - DESCRIBE THE PROBLEM

RUSTY OUTPUT GEAR STATIONARY PIN

On 3/17/13, The Strand Industries Main Plant rejected 17,290 pcs of output gear pins for the presence of rust. The engineering drawing requires the parts to be rust-free. A sample of 50 output gear pins revealed 17 rusty parts, or 34% defective.

8D – An Instructive Example

Purpose of the book:

In this example we are looking at our imaginary firm named MCP Industries. MCP is a direct supplier to Strand Industries, a major OEM. Strand has experienced a quality issue with our product. The complaint is that a small gear mechanism has a rusty output pin. A rejection has been issued against MCP Industries and they have submitted a preliminary 8D based on early investigation of the issue. In this example, MCP Industries has now prepared a full 8D to give to their customer.

This example is intended to be used as a teaching tool for improvement in the elements of 8D problem solving methodology.

There are 8 disciplines in structured problem solving (Thus the term "8D.") In this book, a realistic example is given of each discipline. A section titled "Comments" follows teach example. The comments represent clarification of what is required and it also tells what is unacceptable because certain common actions actually do not contribute to problem solving. These are the "Do's and Don'ts" which are necessary to write a good problem solving report.

Problem solving teams must have a well defined leader. This is a person who will keep the team on track and encourage positive teamwork. A good leader will work his/her way through the 8D steps and ensure that each one is completed correctly.

It is highly recommended that problem solving teams have additional training on the skills used in problem solving such as SPC, Capability, Sampling, Comparison of attribute vs. variables data, measurement error, etc. Without common understanding of these topics, the team may work at cross-purposes.

The table below shows the format for the example within this book. Each of the eight disciplines are discussed in the following order:

Explanation of format for discussing the 8-disciplines

1. Identification of the discipline under discussion
2. An example of the particular step of the 8D
3. Guidance, comments and "Do's and "Don'ts

Each "Discipline" within the 8D process is discussed using a 2-section format as outlined below.

SECTION #1 – on left pages

Presentation of an example which is intended to be a realistic situation. In this case, all examples are relating to a problem which was indentified by our customer. The resulting rejection of an incoming shipment was our first awareness of the issue.

SECTION #2 – on right pages

A listing of *DO's and DON'T's* for each discipline. Also included are helpful comments. This is a very important section and it is aimed at focusing on finding and correcting the root cause of the problem. Special attention is needed to prevent the team from looking making mistakes such as:

1. Erroneously listing symptoms as root causes
2. Failing to fix the root cause (i.e. adding another inspection for example).
3. Neglecting the need to correct the system root cause (i.e. what within the system permitted the root cause to happen and escape our detection?)
4. Seeking to blame others for the problem.

TABLE OF CONTENTS

Subject	Page
1. Use the team approach	5
2. Describe the problem *In customer's terms*	7
3. Containment & short term corrective actions	9
4a. Define and verify root cause *Recognize both the System root cause and the Process root cause*	11
4b. Define and verify root cause (continued)	13
5. Implement and verify permanent corrective Actions	15
6. Implement and verify permanent corrective actions (continued)	17
7. Prevent Recurrence	19
8. Recognize the team	21

APPENDICES

Appendix I	Fishbone Diagram	23
Appendix II	Is/Is-Not Analysis	25
Appendix III	Timeline of Events	27
Author's Notes	Additional discussion	29

#1 EXAMPLE - USE THE TEAM APPROACH

MCP Industries Personnel:

Bill Smith – Champion, Plant Manager
Don Simpson – Engineering Supervisor
Fred Russell – Receiving Inspector
Dave Brill – Grinder Operator – EI Team Leader
Mary Clark – QC Manager
George Jones – Mfg. Superintendent

Sub-Supplier Personnel:

John Brown – QC Manager, Ace Heat Treating
Bob Gardner – Tech Rep – Hi-Tek Coolants
Ann Bowen – Tech. Rep. Fab Steel Co.

Strand Industries Personnel:

Larry James - Strand Ind. Process Engineer
Bill Thompson – Product Design Engineer

#2 COMMENTS

This section must be stated in the customer's terms.

Dates must be stated – start date/end date, including production date of defects.

Frequency and percent defective must be documented

Other quantification includes:

Actual measurements and statistical capability (process potential) estimates.

State clearly what requirements exist. *This includes specifications, standards and other agreements*

5W2H: Who, What, Where, When, Why, How, How Many. It is a good practice to ask "Why" at least 5 times. *Ask "Why until it does not make sense to drill down any deeper.*

Obtain and use specifications, process flow diagrams or other schematics, which show requirements, process, inspection, travel, storage, etc.

Use minimal basic descriptions (i.e.: Rusty output gear pins) and then give a short explanatory paragraph.

Avoid the common mistake of characterizing the problem as follows:

> "The Strand Industries Main Plant found rusty output gear pins......"

The problem is that "We" made the defect, not that the customer found it.

#3 E X A M P L E – CONTAINMENT AND SHORT TERM CORRECTIVE ACTIONS

3/17/13 - All available stock was isolated and sorted with the following results:

Location	Pcs Sorted	Pcs Rejected	Percent Rejected	Confidence
Main Plant	17,290	7,123	41%	95%
Acme	96,500	8,974	9%	95%
HT Treat	38,000	1,486	4%	95%
TOTALS	151,790	17,583	12%	

3/18/13 – Sort Completion (System Purged)

Other Short Term Corrective Actions:

3/18/13 – Added 100% visual inspection at pack line – est. 95% effective.

3/18/13 – Conducted a process audit. Result – All processing parameters were judged to be acceptable to existing process standard.

3/19/13 – Reviewed all raw material in inventory for presence of (a) Undersize, (b) Excess Rust and/or pitting. NONE FOUND

3/19/13 – Reviewed the problem with the Employee Involvement group and involved the EI group in a team brainstorming activity

#3 COMMENTS

It is not necessary to know root cause at this initial time. The first objective is to protect the customer from experiencing any additional defective stock

Containment actions must extend to:

    Your operations

    Your warehouse

    Repair/rework Area

    In-transit stock: *That which is in-transit to and from customer and all sub-suppliers, platers, heat treaters, component sources, finishers, etc.*

What is the % effectiveness of your containment? How was it determined?

List any other short term actions the team has taken (These may be actions taken prior to determining root cause)

What were the dates of the containment actions?

What was found – (this should be quantified)

Audits are not acceptable as containment ACTIONS.

<u>Key Words</u>:

DATA
DATES
QUANTIFICATION
VERIFICATION

#4a E X A M P L E – DEFINE & VERIFY ROOT CAUSE

A Team brainstorming session of 3/17/13 resulted in identification of 3 potential process root causes and 3 potential system root causes as indicated below.

PROCESS ROOT CAUSES:

Priority	Potential Process Root Cause	Estimated % Contribution
1	New Cardboard Dunnage Separators used by Fab Metal Treating Co. have acid residue, that attacks steel.	75%
2	Coolant supplied by Hi-Tek and coolants used by Fab Metal Treating Co. do not inhibit rust.	25%
3	Stock O.D. Size from Fab Steel Co. is not sufficient to allow for "clean-up" during the rough and final grinding operations.	5%

SYSTEM ROOT CAUSES:

Priority	Potential Process Root Cause	Estimated % Contribution
1	Failure to prove-out a process change	75%

#4a COMMENTS

The brainstorming team should have copies of the Fishbone Diagram and the Is/Is-Not analysis on the wall for all to consider in their discussions. These two documents are very helpful in identifying potential root causes. See Appendix I and II for the Fishbone Diagram and the is/is-not analysis.

Keep asking Why, Why, Why?

As we explore each new "Why", we approach closer to the true root cause. We should stop asking "Why" when we begin to consider root causes which are clearly beyond our control (i.e.: Weather, Atmosphere, etc)

Challenge each Root Cause as a symptom or an effect.

Recognize that there is usually a PROCESS root cause and a SYSTEM root cause.

PROCESS root cause: The immediate cause, which acts directly on the manufacturing system.

SYSTEM Root cause: The underlying cause which is within the management system and permits the conditions to exist which result in the process root cause.

The team should jointly determine (or estimate) the contribution of each potential root cause. (See right-hand column in table on prior page)

A fishbone analysis should be considered MANDATORY (This is also referred to as an Ishikawa diagram). See Appendix I for an example.

Is/is-not analysis similarly should be considered MANDATORY. See Appendix II for an example.

#4b. EXAMPLE - DEFINE & VERIFY ROOT CAUSE

VERIFICATION OF ROOT CAUSE:

Cause Ident.	Date	Verification Action	Estimate% Confidence.
P-1	3/18/13	Inspection of the rust pattern on the rejected parts revealed "line" pattern of rust that indicates contact with cardboard separator surfaces	99+%
P-2	3/18/13	A lab chip test using in-process coolant developed rust on chips after 36 hours. The rust protection for this product is 48 hours with no red rust. Additionally, the coolant pH was 6.8 vs. the tech data sheet requires the pH be maintained at 7.1 to 7.3.	100%
P-3	3/19/13	A tolerance stack-up study indicated that minimum stock diameter when coupled with maximum finished output pin diameter, developed the potential for "no clean-up" if pitting or scale is deeper than .002"	25%

#4b C O M M E N T S –(Included in #4a comments.)

For purposes of identifying the category of root cause, the left side of the following examples have codes such as P-1, P-2, S-1, etc. This is to highlight the categorization of the root to "Process" or to "System." As added root causes are considered, they are numbered sequentially within each category. Also, beneath these codes there is a label such as "Prevention" or "Detection." This is identification of the corrective actions as either working on preventing the concern or merely detecting it. Prevention actions can significantly lower costs while Detection actions keep a lot of non-value added costs within the process.

#5/6a. EXAMPLE – IMPLEMENT AND VERIFY PERMANENT CORRECTIVE ACTIONS

VERIFICATION OF
PERMANENT CORRECTIVE ACTIONS:

Cause Ident.	Date	Corrective Actions	Estimate % Confidence
P-1 (Prevention)	3/20/13	Resin coated white cardboard were reinstated in production. These are the same separators as used prior to the problem. This material has been added to the process sheets and specified on the bill of materials.	99+%
P-2 (Prevention)	3/20/13	The in-process coolant will be monitored daily for pH and adjusted or discarded when it drops below pH 7.1. The PFMEA has been changed to reflect the pH controls.	99+%
P-3 (Prevention)	3/24/13	All bar material was re-specified to be purchased at .003" larger stock diameter.	100%
S-1 (Prevention)	3/20/13	The Fab Ht Treat Co. procedures were modified to require prove-out of all significant process changes	95%
S-2 (System)	3/26/13	The characteristic of "rust" has been added to the dock audit instruction sheet. The results will be logged in the Dock Audit record sheet	95%
S-3 (System)	4/1/13	FMEA Updated	100%

#5/6a COMMENTS

Label each action to identify the PROCESS or SYSTEM root cause it is acting on (This permits an "accounting" system to ensure each cause has an action directed toward it)

Identify whether each action is PREVENTION or DETECTION. (The best and lost cost solution involves the use of preventive actions)

QOS reporting systems are an excellent source of verification data. Also use SPC charts, Cpk's, Ppk's, before and after the fix. ("…the Cpk was 0.53 prior to the fix and 1.8 after the corrective action – studies attached as back-up)
Another example: "Prior to actions, throughput losses were 1.36%. After the 3/11/13 fix, the process throughput losses were 0.04% - as per attached Percent defective (Rust) chart."

DO NOT rely on your customer for verification !. (i.e.: Avoid statements like the following: "The Strand Industries Main Plant receiving inspection did not reject any more shipments.")

Is the timing, frequency, and % defective consistent with the stated root cause?

We would expect to see the customer data in the Paynter chart as a part of the verification, but it should only supplement other data (i.e.: see above DO NOT rely on your customer for verification)

#5/6b. EXAMPLE – IMPLEMENT AND VERIFY PERMANENT CORRECTIVE ACTIONS

VERIFICATION OF CORRECTIVE ACTIONS

Paynter Chart
Showing Percent Defective (Rust) by Date with Pareto Chart

			D A T E			
Location	3/5	3/12	3/19	3/26	4/2	4/9
FAB HT	N/A	41%	21%	0%	0%	0%
Strand Ind.	0%	1.2%	3.7%	0%	0%	0%

Note: Containment actions implemented 3/22/13

KEY: FAB / STRAND

Sort Results: Defects (Rust) found by date of production

5-Mar		12-Mar		19-Mar		26-Mar		2-Apr		9-Apr	
0%	0%	41%	1.2%	21%	3.7%	0%	0%	0%	0%	0%	0%

Note: Containment actions implemented 3/22/13

#5/6b COMMENTS

A Paynter chart is an effective display of data for the purpose of convincing your customer that containment and permanent corrective actions have been implemented. A Paynter Chart is simply a run chart with a Pareto Chart.

To illustrate a few actions directed toward root cause, consider an additional example in which the defect is breakage of plastic snap tabs on a plastic part determined to be the result of excessive stress.

Potential actions directed toward the true root cause:

Eliminate the Root Cause (i.e.: "tabs break" – redesign to eliminate stress by moving the tabs to other areas

Do an "end run" on the root cause. (i.e.: Eliminate tabs)

Design for robustness (i.e.: make tabs bigger, stronger, better stress loading, compliance, etc)

Actions toward the System Root Cause:

Update the DV plan to find this condition when it is under development.

Update the process sheets to include a check for broken tabs

Revise the DVP&R to include a requirement for tab robustness.

Other considerations:

> Once actions are recommended ask the team the following questions:
>
> Do these actions make sense when reviewing the root causes listed in section #4?
>
> Do these actions adequately cover the location, timing, and magnitude as listed in the problem statement?

#7   EXAMPLE - PREVENT RECURRENCE

3/20/13 – The PFMEA was revised to add RUST as a concern with the following RPN Weights

```
SEVERITY =     6
DETECTION =    5
OCCURRENCE =   5
     RPN = 150 (6x5x5)
```

As noted above, permanent preventive actions were implemented on each of the process and system root causes.

#7 COMMENTS

Be sure to explore all necessary modifications to management and operating systems

Also consider all necessary modifications to practices and procedures.

The actions must be directed toward the Root Cause(s)

IMPORTANT – THE FOLLOWING ITEMS ARE NOT ALLOWED AS PREVENTIVE ACTIONS:

Detection Actions

Audits

Inspections

#8. EXAMPLE - RECOGNIZE THE TEAM

This could be anything from a short note of closure to a formal note in someone's personnel file recognizing both the individual's contribution and the spirit of the team approach.

For people outside of your immediate organization, this could be a business luncheon or if the contribution was "above and beyond," it could be notes to people's immediate supervisors.

#8 COMMENTS

Recognize the team effort.

Recognize the individual contributions

Document the efforts

Add the lessons learned to the organization knowledge base
    Significant/Critical Characteristics
PFMEA
    Process Sheets
    Design Guides
    FMEA
    Other…

Report to Management

Appendix I – Fishbone Diagram Example

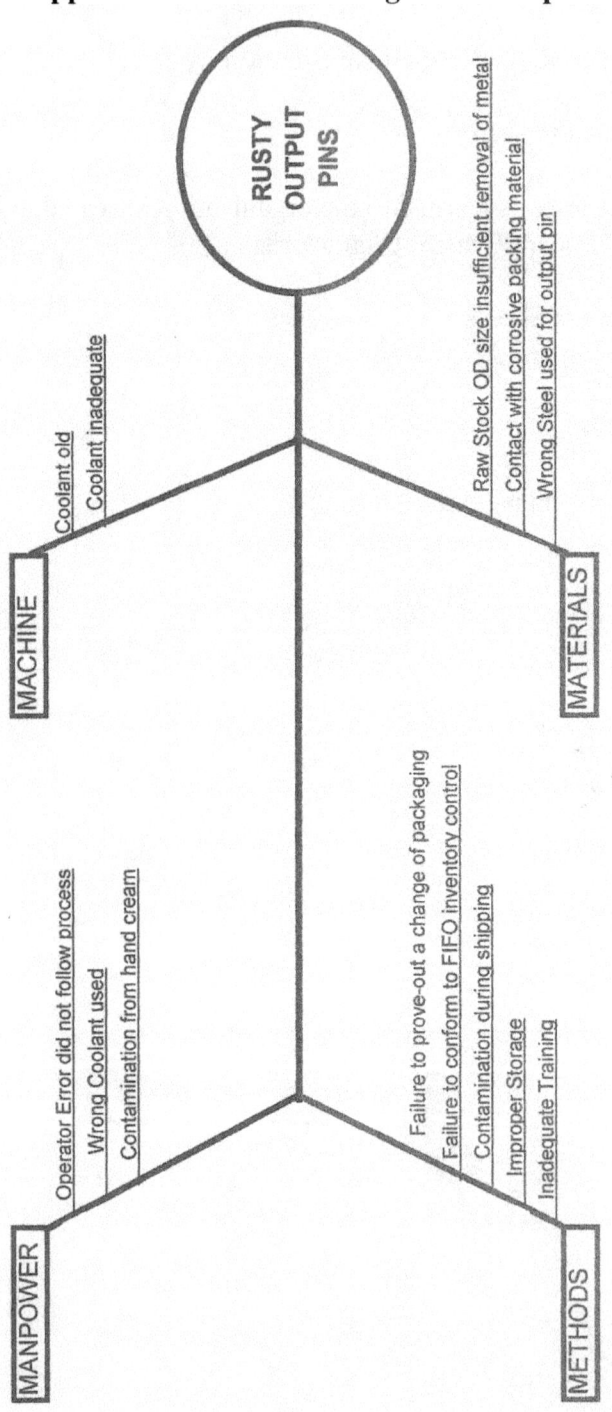

Appendix I – Comments on the Fishbone Diagram Example

The following illustration depicts the output of a team brainstorming effort as described in the section titled "#4a – DEFINE & VERIFY ROOT CAUSE.

As early as possible after team formation, the team leader should conduct a brainstorming session. During the brainstorming, the team leader presents an empty diagram with the problem in the circle and the "4M's" are already in the diagram: Manpower, Machine, Methods, and Materials. As an option, the team leader can suggest other general areas to include in the boxed areas of this diagram. Other areas such as Environment etc. could be added if the team felt it were necessary to facilitate brainstorming.

This session usually takes 1 to 2 hours to complete. It is most effective when knowledgeable people from all departments and areas which could have input in either correcting or verifying the problem under review. It is mandatory that group leader establish a relaxed climate free of fear of speaking out. The two most important rules are (1) Everyone contributes, even if it is a verbal "I don't know." and (2) No criticism. While it is ok to challenge input if you have added knowledge, but do not allow personal attacks or general negative statements.

All ideas should be put on the Fishbone diagram. After development of the Fishbone Diagram, the next step is to prioritize these POTENTIAL root causes.

Appendix II – Is/Is-Not Analysis

Rusty Output Pin		
IS	IS NOT	MAY BE
First observed 3/17/13 by Customer	Observed before 3/17/13	May have existed undetected in past
12% defective	100% defective	Other defect rates
	Found in Main Plant	Due to storage or transit
	Not a raw material issue	Packaging (new cardboard)
		Stock ID size (insufficient metal removal)
		Coolants - insufficient rust inhibitor

Appendix II – Comments on the Is/Is-Not Analysis

This is an optional exercise and it can be extremely useful. This is usually prepared by 1 or 2 individuals who have the most knowledge of the specific issue being investigated.

The Is/Is-Not Analysis should be completed before the brainstorming session and either displayed for the team to see or else given to team members as a handout.

The first 5-10 minutes of the brainstorming session should be devoted to a review and revision of the Is/Is-not analysis when all the team members can give their inputs.

Appendix III – Timeline

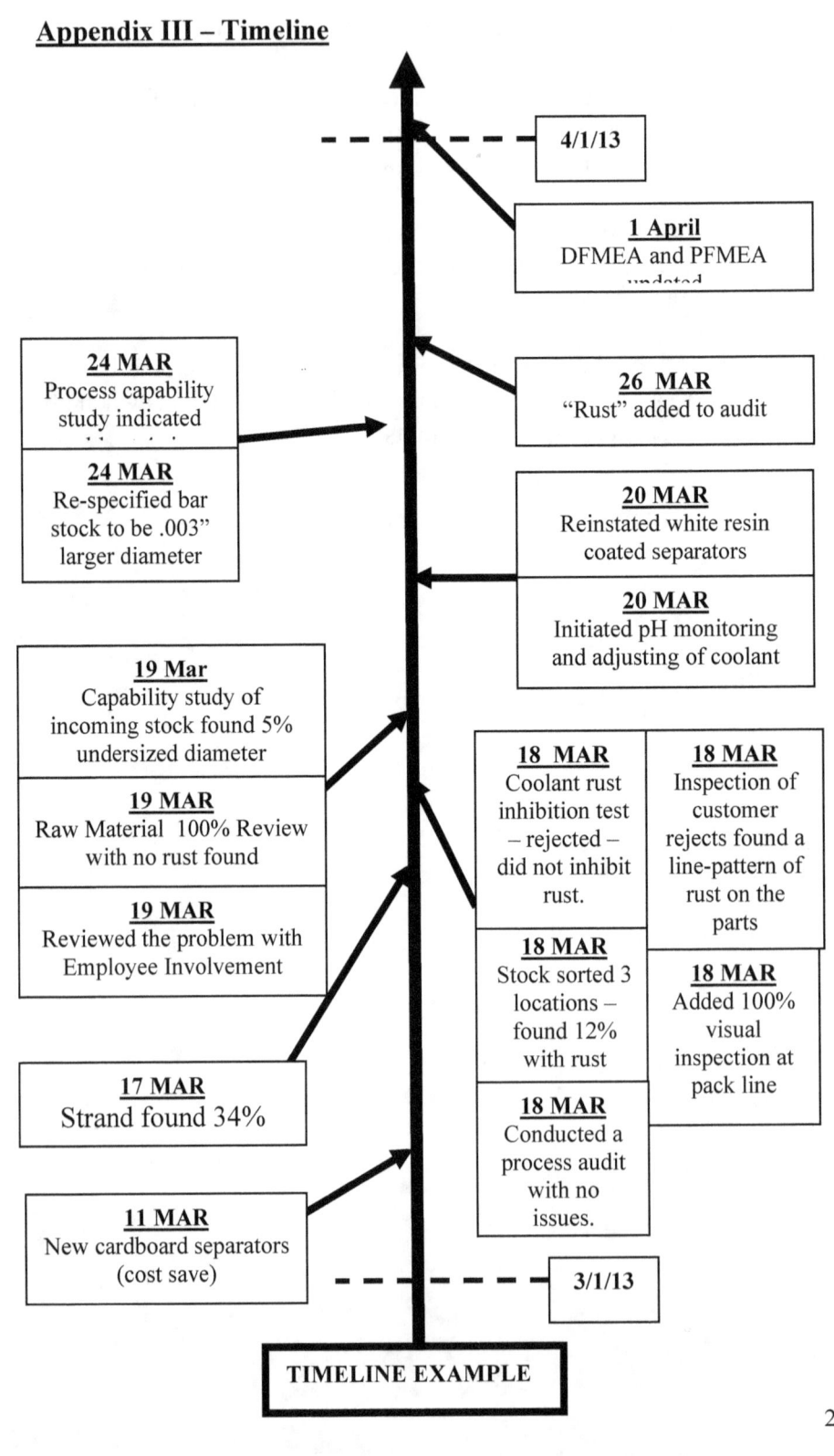

Appendix III– Comments on the Timeline

Similar to the Is/Is-Not Analysis, the Timeline analysis can also be extremely useful, especially for complicated issues.

Again, his is usually prepared by 1 or 2 individuals who have the most knowledge of the specific issue being investigated.

Also, the Timeline should either be displayed or handed to the team members on a printed form. The review and revision of the Timeline should be conducted at the same time as the review of the Is/Is-Not analysis.

Authors Notes:

How many times should we ask WHY?

In reality, the quest for "why" should stop when it gets to things totally out of anyone's control. For an oversimplified example, consider that we were working on the problem of "The picture fell off the wall hanger." If we asked "Why?" until we got down to GRAVITY, we are obviously wasting our time. This seems trivial, but there are many environmental factors which, if listed as root cause, which is out of our control and would not lead to a solution. Typically, we protect from such a cause rather than fix them. For example:

> *We buy a picture hanger rated for this specific picture*
>
> *We make sure the wall is correct for the picture hanger*
>
> *We make sure the picture hanger is installed correctly*

The importance of a team effort

This can not be emphasized enough. It has been proven repeatedly that when people solve problems, the best individual effort is not as good as the worst effort by a proper team.

Formation of the team

The comments in section I (Use the Team Approach) cover this. However, here are some reinforcements that should be made.

Make a special effort to include people who <u>want</u> to work on the problem. Avoid those few people in the organization who are chronic complainers or otherwise have demonstrated an agenda not consistent with working within a team.

Who are the "Customers" in this issue?
Recognize that there are customers and suppliers within each organization. The Receiving Department is a Customer of both the supplier and the logistics firm. Additionally, the Receiving Department is a supplier to the Manufacturing Floor. The

Manufacturing floor is a supplier to the Shipping Department. This reciprocal relationship takes place within all organizations.

Guard against "Groupthink."

This is a phenomenon in which individuals feel the organizational pressure to an extent they are more focused on trying to please the boss or otherwise insecure about the political ramifications of saying what they think. Some organizations with powerful leaders who tend to be "Top-down" type of managers make sure that such people are excluded from the team. In this case, it would be a good idea to begin the meeting by talking about groupthink as a possible detriment. Everyone should be made to feel comfortable in expressing their ideas. This is more important when some people see flaws in the system or product but have been rebuked by their co-workers, supervisors, or managers when they try to discuss these issues.

Be a Bulldog on containment

One of the most common causes of a repeat problem is failure to contain. Everyone can easily see the obvious areas to perform containment:

The manufacturing operation

The customer's Receiving Dock

The customer's Manufacturing Floor

There are, however many other considerations which could contain product which should be evaluated:

Stock which has been put on hold for other considerations

Stock which is within a rework or repair process (Separate from the direct manufacturing operation)

Parts in shipment

Parts stored in distribution centers or warehouses, especially when these locations are at a remote location.

Customer returns for this reason or other reasons. (The "other reason" category is especially dangerous and must be evaluated).

"Show and Tell" parts which have been used for meetings, discussions or other illustrative purposes.

* * * * * * * * * * * * * *

I hope you will find this book helpful. If you have recommendations for corrections or otherwise to improve it, please let me know.
mcpoz@comcast.net

www.ingramcontent.com/pod-product-compliance
Lightning Source LLC
Chambersburg PA
CBHW061522180526
45171CB00001B/289